D0753316

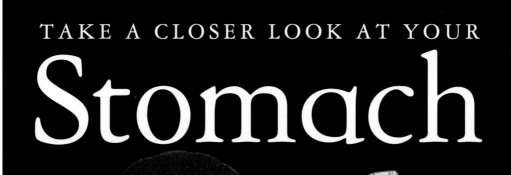

TAKE A CLOSER LOOK AT YOUR
Stomach

BY JANE P. GARDNER

The Child's World

Published by The Child's World®
1980 Lookout Drive • Mankato, MN 56003-1705
800-599-READ • www.childsworld.com

Acknowledgments
The Child's World®: Mary Berendes, Publishing Director
Red Line Editorial: Editorial direction and production
The Design Lab: Design
Content Consultant: Jeffrey W. Oseid, MD

Photographs ©: Ingram Publishing/Thinkstock, title; Tom Le
Goff/Thinkstock, title, 23; Artville, title; Shutterstock Images,
5, 9, 11, 17; Brand X Pictures, 7, 20, 24; Alila Sao Mai/
Shutterstock Images, 13, 14; Karen Sarraga/Shutterstock
Images, 15; Kasia Bialasiewicz/Shutterstock Images, 19;
Monkey Business/Thinkstock, 21

Front cover: Ingram Publishing/Thinkstock; Tom Le Goff/
Thinkstock; Artville

ISBN 978-1623235536
LCCN 2013931445

Printed in the United States of America
Mankato, MN
July, 2013
PA02175

About the Author

Jane P. Gardner is a freelance science writer with a master's degree in geology. She worked as a science teacher for several years before becoming a science writer. She has written textbooks, tests, laboratory experiments, and other books on biology, health, environmental science, chemistry, geography, earth science, and math.

Table of Contents

CHAPTER 1

What Is the Stomach?

What did you have for breakfast? Did you have eggs and toast or cereal and milk? Maybe you had pancakes and sausage. No matter what you ate, your food is settling in your stomach. Soon the food will keep moving through your digestive system. This system helps break down your food. It also takes in nutrients from your food.

The stomach is an organ in the digestive system. This system is about 30 feet (9 m) long. The digestive system is a series of tubes. Other organs are part of the digestive system, too. These organs include the **small intestine** and the **esophagus**.

The stomach is a pouch and looks like the letter J. It is made of muscles that get bigger and smaller. Your stomach muscles are **involuntary** muscles. This means they work without you having to think about them.

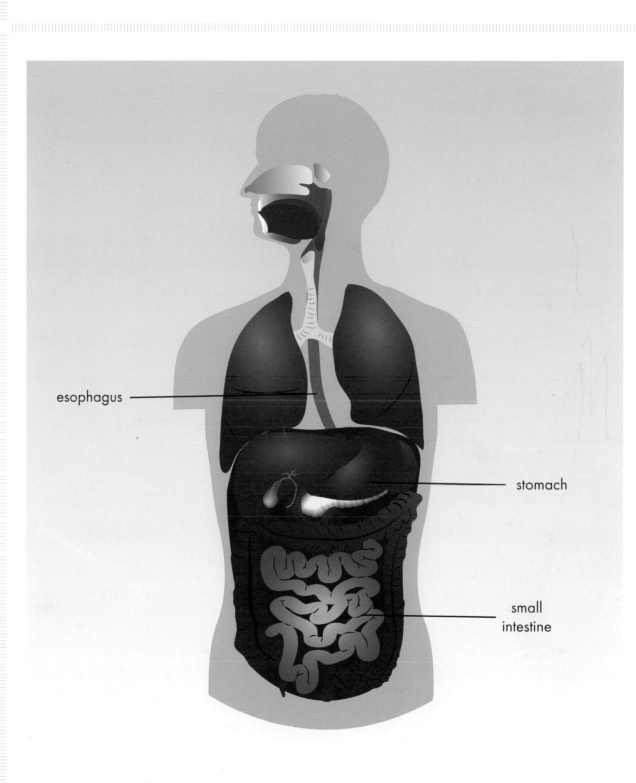

esophagus

stomach

small
intestine

Your food makes many stops as it travels through the digestive system.

An empty stomach is about the size of your fist. It can expand to almost ten times as big! The stomach can hold about 2 quarts (2 L) of food. This is the size of a medium pizza!

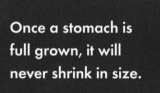

Once a stomach is full grown, it will never shrink in size.

The stomach is between the esophagus and the small intestine. Food moves from the esophagus into the stomach in four to eight seconds. That is some fast-moving breakfast! Food goes through a set of muscles before entering the stomach. These muscles close so food does not move back into the esophagus.

Food begins to break down in the stomach. It then moves into the small intestine. Nutrients from the food are stored in the stomach for the body's energy.

Food travels through your esophagus until it settles in your stomach.

CHAPTER 2

What Does the Stomach Do?

Try this activity: place a few crackers in a plastic bag. Break the crackers into small pieces. Carefully open the bag and add a few drops of water. Close the bag and continue to break the crumbs. Do you notice how the crumbs have turned into goo? This is similar to what your stomach does to food you eat.

The stomach has three jobs. It stores food the body cannot use right away. This food is saved until the body is ready to use it.

The second job of the stomach is to break down food. The stomach muscles mix the food in the stomach. This movement breaks the food into smaller pieces. The stomach also has **gastric juices**. These juices are made of salt and acid. The acid works to break down the food more. Eventually the food forms into goo called **chyme**.

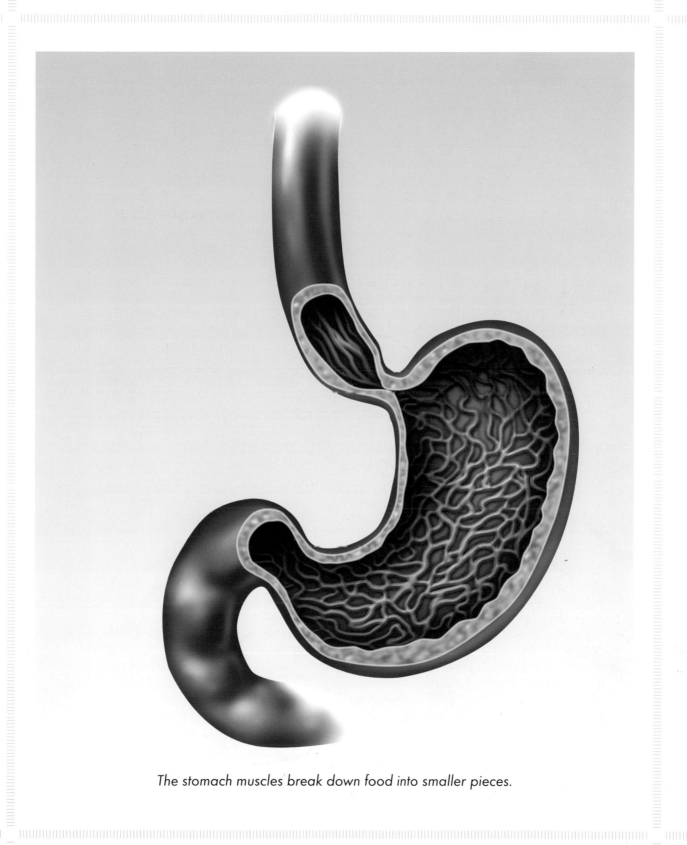

The stomach muscles break down food into smaller pieces.

The stomach lining is very strong. The acids could break down the stomach without the lining.

The third job of the stomach is to move the chyme. The stomach muscles push the chyme into the small intestine. Food empties slowly into the small intestine. On average it takes about four to five hours. The length depends on three factors. It depends on the type of food and how healthy you are. It also depends on how much water you have had during the day.

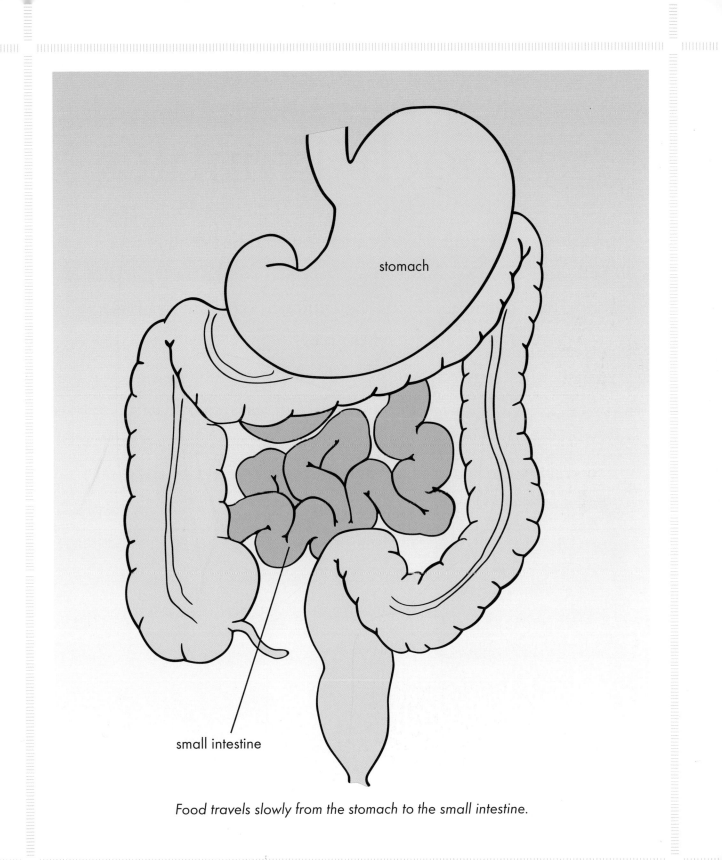

stomach

small intestine

Food travels slowly from the stomach to the small intestine.

CHAPTER 3
Stomach Troubles

Sometimes your stomach does not feel well. Most of the time, a bellyache is not serious. But sometimes it can be something more. There are many things that can cause tummy troubles.

Acid reflux disease is common. It can be a problem for anyone, even babies. Acid reflux happens when stomach acid gets back into the esophagus. Heartburn usually follows. It is a burning feeling in the stomach, chest, or throat. Acid reflux can be treated with medication. Changing your eating habits might also help.

Sometimes stomachs growl or make rumbling noises. This might mean you're hungry. But it can also happen after eating or in between meals when food is being digested.

Acid Reflux

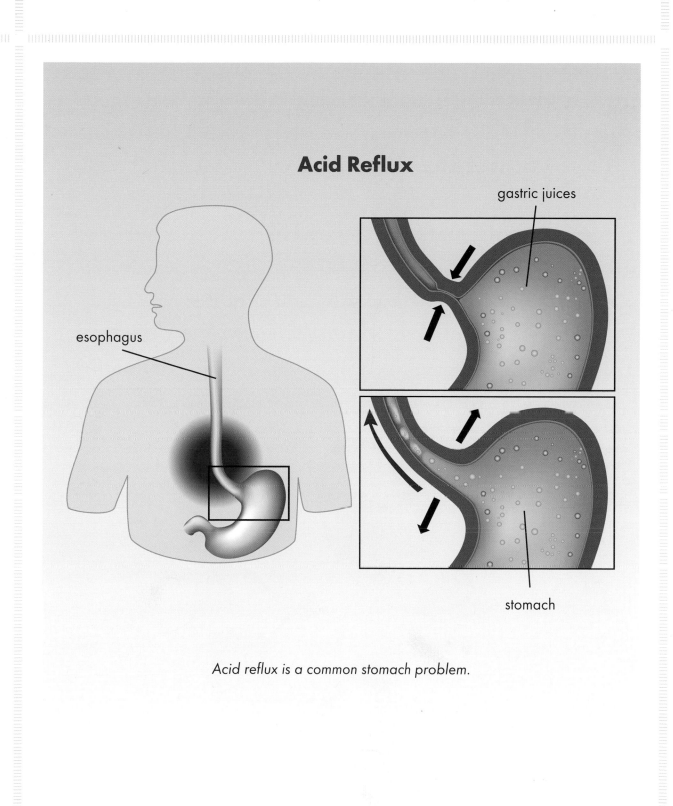

esophagus

gastric juices

stomach

Acid reflux is a common stomach problem.

An **ulcer** is a sore inside the stomach. Stomach acid irritates the ulcer. This can be painful. Some people feel sick from ulcers. They might also feel either hungry or full.

People used to think **stress** caused ulcers. Doctors now know **bacteria** cause most ulcers. Many people have bacteria in their stomachs. Not everyone will get an ulcer. Bad habits like smoking can lead to ulcers. Some medications or sicknesses can also cause ulcers. Many people with ulcers are given **antibiotics**. The antibiotics try to treat the bacteria causing the ulcer.

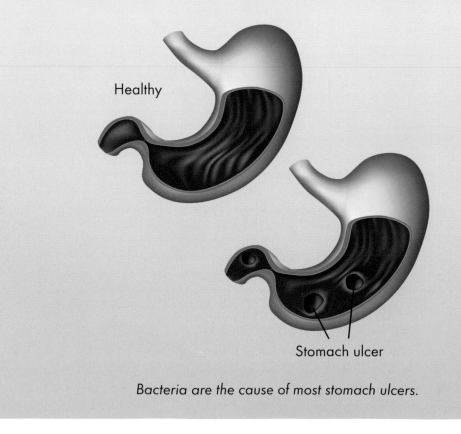

Healthy

Stomach ulcer

Bacteria are the cause of most stomach ulcers.

Problems in the stomach can cause some food allergies. Sometimes a person's stomach does not have enough acid. This means the stomach cannot break down all the food. Other people develop food allergies. People can be allergic to food like nuts, milk, or wheat. You should not eat foods if you are allergic to them.

Some people are allergic to dairy products, such as milk and cheese.

A common stomach problem is the stomach flu. The stomach flu is **contagious**. It can spread easily from person to person. You might have stomach pains when you have the flu. Sometimes you might even throw up. Throwing up is not fun, but it helps you feel better. Throwing up helps your stomach get rid of the germs.

Food poisoning also makes you throw up. Food poisoning comes from eating bad food. The food might have germs or bad bacteria. Eating bad bacteria will make your stomach upset. Throwing up the bad germs will help your stomach feel better.

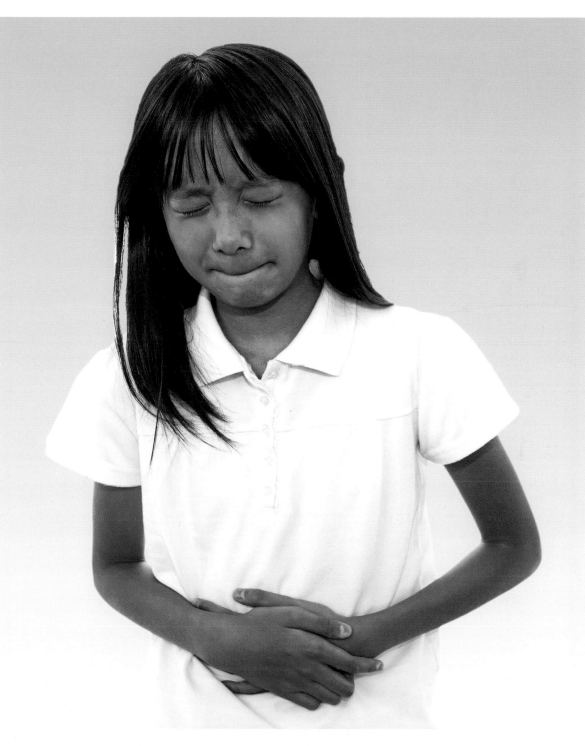

Your stomach might hurt when you have the stomach flu or food poisoning.

CHAPTER 4

Keeping Your Stomach Healthy

"You are what you eat!" You may have heard your mom or dad say this. Eating healthy food helps you live a healthier life. Your body will not feel well if you only eat junk food. The foods you eat will keep your stomach healthy.

Eating a lot of **fiber** can help your stomach digest food. Fruits like apples, bananas, and raspberries have fiber. Whole wheat pastas and brown rice are also good choices. Vegetables like peas, broccoli, and corn also have fiber. Eating lots of food with fiber is good for your stomach.

Eating healthy foods will help keep your stomach healthy.

Your stomach needs a lot of water to work well. Drink a lot of fluids each day. Be sure to avoid sugary drinks like soda or sports drinks. Water and unsweetened juices are the best.

Eating yogurt can help with digestion. Yogurt also helps your stomach break down the chemicals in milk products.

Choosing healthy snacks like yogurt keeps your stomach healthy.

Chew your food well before you swallow. Breaking food into smaller pieces is also good. This will give your stomach a head start on its job. Eat slowly. Try to avoid greasy foods as much as possible. If you are what you eat, then you should eat healthy foods to keep yourself healthy.

Eating too fast can bring gas into your stomach. It needs to get rid of that gas. The stomach pushes the gas out of your body as a burp!

Eating slowly and chewing carefully will help your stomach do its job.

GLOSSARY

antibiotics (an-ti-bye-OT-iks) Antibiotics are drugs used to cure infections and diseases. Antibiotics can be taken to treat a stomach ulcer.

bacteria (bak-TIHR-ee-uh) Bacteria are microscopic living things that are all around you. Bacteria cause most stomach ulcers.

chyme (KAHYM) Chyme is partially liquefied food in the stomach. The stomach moves chyme into the small intestine.

contagious (kuhn-TAY-juhss) A contagious disease can be spread from person to person. The stomach flu is contagious.

esophagus (i-SOF-uh-guhss) The esophagus is an organ in the digestive system. Food moves through the esophagus into the stomach.

fiber (FYE-bur) Fiber is a nutrient that helps food move through the intestines. Fruits, vegetables, and whole wheat pasta have fiber.

gastric juices (GASS-trik JOOS-uhz) Gastric juices are the fluids in the stomach. Gastric juices are made of salt and acid.

involuntary (in-VOL-uhn-ter-ee) To have no control over something is involuntary. The stomach is made up of involuntary muscles.

small intestine (SMAWL in-TESS-tin) The small intestine is an organ in the digestive system. Most food is broken down in the small intestine.

stress (STRESS) Stress is being worried about something. Stress may lead to stomach ulcers.

ulcer (UHL-sur) An ulcer is a sore on the inside of the stomach. Bacteria in the stomach can create an ulcer.

LEARN MORE

BOOKS

Simon, Seymour. *Guts: Our Digestive System*. New York: Harper Collins, 2005.

Taylor-Butler, Christine. *The Digestive System*. New York: Children's Press, 2008.

WEB SITES

Visit our Web site for links about the stomach: **childsworld.com/links**

Note to Parents, Teachers, and Librarians: We routinely verify our Web links to make sure they are safe and active sites. So encourage your readers to check them out!

INDEX